HOW TO
RESPOND
WHEN YOU FEEL
MISTREATED

John Bevere

NELSON BOOKS
A Division of Thomas Nelson Publishers
Since 1798

www.thomasnelson.com

All Scripture quotations, unless otherwise indicated, are taken from the New King James Version®. Copyright © 1982 by Thomas Nelson, Inc. Used by permission. All rights reserved.

Scripture quotations noted NLT are from the *Holy Bible*, NEW LIVING TRANSLATION, Copyright © 1996. Used by permission of Tyndale House Publishers, Inc., Wheaton, Illinois 60189. All rights reserved.

Scripture quotations noted AMPLIFIED BIBLE are from THE AMPLIFIED BIBLE: Old Testament. Copyright © 1962, 1964 by Zondervan Publishing House (used by permission); and from THE AMPLIFIED NEW TESTAMENT. Copyright © 1958 by the Lockman Foundation (used by permission).

Library of Congress Cataloging-in-Publication Data

How to respond when you feel mistreated / John Bevere.
    p. cm.
   ISBN: 0-7852-6000-5 (hardcover)
   1. International conflict—Religious aspects—Christianity. 2. Submissiveness—Religious aspects—Christianity. I. Title.
BV4597.53.C58B48 2004
248.4—dc22   2004011434

Printed in the United States of America

04 05 06 07 08 QW 5 4 3 2

Contents

1

An Ignored Truth

Have you ever been mistreated?

If you answered "No," I want you to check your pulse! It's possible you are no longer with us! For the truth is that to live in our fallen, broken, sinful world is to face multiple opportunities every day to be mistreated and not receive the just and fair treatment we all desire.

There are many situations in which a person can receive bad treatment. Here are a few possibilities—I'm sure you could add to the list:

- If you are a child—of any age—you might have a parent who constantly criticizes you unfairly.

- Or if you are a parent, you may have a rebellious or prodigal child who gives you insults and disobedience instead of love.

- You may be a student who just can't please a demanding teacher.

- You may be a great employee, but your boss doesn't like you and wants to force you out of your job—to give it to one of her friends.

- You are driving your car and obeying the speed limit. But the driver behind you is in a hurry, blows his horn, gives you an obscene gesture, and curses as he drives by.

- You own your own business and treat customers well. But a competitor undercuts your prices and accuses you of shoddy work.

- You have been married for fifteen years, during which you put your husband through college and bore him three children. He just told you he doesn't love you anymore and wants to marry a coworker.

- You have served in your church as a deacon, but your passion is leading the youth choir. You were just told that the choir will now be led by the new pastor's wife.

These are just a few possible scenarios. There are certainly thousands more. No one is immune. The rich and strong receive it just like the poor and powerless. Some mistreatment is laughably minor. Other acts are horrific, having the power to wreck a person's reputation—and even to threaten life itself.

But now let me share with you a truth from God's heart that too many people do not know or choose to ignore: *If we allow God to handle those who mistreat us, we will mature and reap great blessings.* That's what this book is about. If you are tired of the frustration that can come from not knowing how to respond to the poor treatment you receive from others, you are in for a wonderful revelation: God sees your suffering, He understands your suffering, and He's got plans to bring tremendous good out of it in your life. But you need to know how He wants you to do that. And then you must get with His program and obey.

The results: a maturity, a strength, an opportunity to participate strategically in advancing the kingdom of God. You may not believe me now, but by the time I finish sharing this incredible truth from God's Word, you will understand why, when mistreatment comes your way, that's the time to let out a shout of joy and dance a jig. It's time for a party in your soul! You are about to participate in one of God's key efforts here on earth to show His faithfulness to His children and bring about great victories over the evil, destructive plans of the enemy.

But I admit the normal way too many people respond to mistreatment is to get angry and seek to get even. We live in a world where God's intentions have been twisted, sometimes almost beyond recognition. One of His great, foundational, spiritual laws is the notion of justice. Built into our very mental and emotional foundation is a strong sense of right and wrong. So when we are wronged, we want somebody, somewhere, to make things right. Often we think that means us. That's wrong.

Several years ago our son Addison experienced an injustice at school. What happened, and how he responded, reveals the key, life-changing principles I will explain in this book.

There may be nothing worse than seeing your child mistreated. As a father of four boys, in my flesh the first thing I want to do when one of them is wronged is to rise up immediately and go settle the score. It's one of those "let's act first and talk later" kind of sinful responses.

> So when we are wronged, we want somebody, somewhere, to make things right. Often we think that means us. That's wrong.

That's how I felt as day after day, our oldest son, Addison, came home and told us about the bad things happening at school. My wife, Lisa, and I sat each night and listened as nine-year-old Addison shared story after story of how his teacher picked on him. This just didn't seem right because Addison always had been a good student and was attending a fine Christian school. Just what was happening to turn our son into such a grumbler and complainer?

Lisa and I had talked privately about this a number of times. We really could not figure it out. Addison was all boy, but normally he did not get into trouble. For some reason the teacher often assumed that if there was trouble in the class, Addison was the instigator. The whole class could be goofing off, but when it came time to let the hammer down, the teacher usually singled out Addison and railed on him. The best answer Lisa and I could come up with was that it must be a personality clash. Maybe

Addison and his teacher just didn't hit it off. Sometimes that happens.

We prayed about this and hoped the situation would improve. It didn't. God wanted to answer our prayers, and eventually He did. But it took a while because Addison needed to learn firsthand how the Lord wants His children to respond to mistreatment.

The straw that broke Addison's little back, though, happened one day when two of his classmates—who sat behind him—were joking around. The teacher's back was to the class, but when he turned around to correct the situation, the boys quickly quieted down. Without missing a beat, the teacher started yelling at Addison. Like everyone else, Addison hates injustice. As a result of being falsely accused of goofing off in class, his heart was wounded.

Addison came home that night and told Lisa and me what had happened. We sat at the dinner table, and big alligator tears poured from his eyes as he sobbed. This was a big deal for a third grader. Good mom that she is, Lisa took him in her arms and held him, saying over and over, "Oh, my son, my son!" I felt bad, too, and I racked my brain—*What could I do? What should I tell my son?*

While Lisa continued comforting him, something inside my spirit didn't feel right—the Holy Spirit was giving me a nudge. Then I remembered a lesson I had learned years before. A light-bulb turned on in my mind, and I knew clearly what I needed to say to my son.

"Well, Addison, can I ask you something?" I said. He was

still whimpering, huddled next to Lisa. "How did you respond when your teacher did that to you today?"

Addison straightened up, and I saw fire ignite in his eyes. "I told him it wasn't me; it was those other two guys!" he said fiercely.

"Do you always do that when he corrects you?" I asked.

"Yeah, especially if he's wrong, which is most of the time!"

"Son, what you're doing is not right," I answered. I picked up my Bible and read him some key verses. I reminded him of how Jesus had faced bad treatment. I also told him a story of how I had been mistreated as a pastor.

"Addison, you have a choice," I said finally. "You can continue to defend yourself and keep resisting authority, or you can do this God's way, which I think means you should go to your teacher and ask forgiveness for constantly challenging his authority and his decisions. Take your pick."

"But Dad, suppose the teacher's wrong?"

"Well, Addison, has your way worked?"

"No."

"Then you have a choice. You can follow Jesus' example like the Bible says, or you can do this yourself."

"Okay, I'll do it God's way," Addison said.

"All right, let's pray." So we prayed.

The next day Addison made an appointment to see his teacher at lunchtime. He looked at the teacher and said, "Sir, God has dealt with me. I have constantly challenged your authority. That's wrong. Would you please forgive me? I will not do this anymore."

As you can imagine, that blew the teacher away. The end of

the next week, guess to whom the teacher gave the Student of the Week award?

Addison.

And to top it off, at the end of the year the teacher gave an Outstanding Student for the Year award. Do I need to tell you who won?

Addison.

My question is: If handling mistreatment as God commands works for a third grader, do you think it just might work for you and me?

What I intend to do in this book, with the help of the Holy Spirit, is arm you to respond to mistreatment in a way that will bring you great blessing.

As you may know, my ministry involves speaking almost on a weekly basis at churches and conferences in the United States and throughout the world. As I talk to people and discern what's on their hearts, overwhelmingly I am hearing that vast numbers of Christians are being tested by hard things in their lives. Throughout the past year I've frequently asked during my messages, "For how many of you was the last year the toughest you have ever faced?" From 75 to 90 percent of those in attendance have raised their hands! This is just unprecedented in my experience. I believe God is up to something phenomenal.

Dr. Yongi Cho once said it this way:

I've got to die a thousand deaths before God begins to do something new in my life. One day I asked the Lord, "Why do I have to die one thousand deaths?"

The Lord replied, "Because you have to have the character to handle what I'm about to place in you as far as responsibility goes."

Often the hard things and suffering we face involve mistreatment by others. That's why I believe God has given me this message to share with you in this book.

Once after I had given my message on how to respond to unfair treatment, a man in the audience—a teacher at a Bible school—was so ministered to by the content that he went home and listened to the message on tape eleven times. He told me that he turned the material into an academic course called "Christianity 101" because he believed every Christian needs to know how to respond to unfair treatment but hardly anyone receives teaching on this topic.

Here is what God promises to do on your behalf if you respond well to mistreatment:

- He will defend and vindicate you.

- He will bountifully bless you.

- You will grow in character and develop your spiritual muscles.

Let's find out how all of this can come about in your life—to your benefit, the advancement of the kingdom of God, and—most important—to the glory of God.

2

Vengeance Is His

I was far beyond third grade when I learned that it is better to let the Lord handle matters of injustice when you are being treated unfairly.

Early in my ministry I was a youth pastor at a large church of about eight thousand members. My supervisor was an administrative pastor who in turn reported to the senior pastor.

I loved the job. God had put a fire in my heart to give those young men and women the truth from His Word in as clear a way as possible. So my weekly messages to them were not fluff. I taught them about obedience to God, holiness, the crucified life, how to go into the prayer closet and approach God boldly—topics like that. Each Tuesday night I hit those 250 kids hard, and they were eating it up.

My boss's fifteen-year-old son was in the youth group. God was touching this young man, and he was catching fire in his walk with Christ. After several months this young man approached Lisa one night with tears running down his face. With his voice cracking he said, "Miss Lisa, how can I live the godly life that Pastor

John is preaching about every week, when in my own home my mom and dad are doing things that are just not right?" He then gave Lisa some details.

Lisa was shocked, because this was my boss the young man was describing. "Listen, this is not about what your mom and dad are doing," Lisa told him. "Your life is between Jesus and you. What Pastor John is preaching, you just live that life before God. How your mom and dad live is not your responsibility. Just leave them with the Lord, pray for them, and respect them." That was about all Lisa could think of to say, but it was wise advice.

I don't know if Lisa's encounter with the young man and what happened next were connected or not, but about this time my boss, the administrative pastor, started making life very difficult for me. I learned that he was telling the senior pastor things about me that were not true. And at the same time he was reporting things to me that the senior pastor supposedly was saying about me. A chasm was forming between the senior pastor and me; it was obvious that my boss's agenda was to get rid of me.

A few months went by until after a youth service one night four of my students came up to me—two of them with tears in their eyes. "Pastor John," one of them blurted out, "we can't believe you're getting fired!"

"Excuse me?" I said. "Where did you hear this?" It took me a few minutes to find out that the rumor had originated with the administrative pastor's son. So I decided to have a talk with him. "Where did you hear I was getting fired?" I asked the teenager.

"From my dad."

That did it! I made an appointment and went in to see my boss. "I have something alarming to ask you about," I told him. "I had several young people come up to me at youth group and tell me I'm getting fired, and I traced the story back to your son. He told me he heard this from you. What's going on?"

The man squirmed in his chair. "Well, John, I'm so sorry. I was only repeating to my wife the other day what the senior pastor was saying about you, and my son must have overheard it. I'm so sorry. I'll tell him not to say these things anymore." He didn't offer any additional explanation.

"Well, thanks," I said and left his office. Now I really was confused. I didn't know if I was coming or going.

This uncertainty hung over me like a black cloud for another two months. Finally, some other men on staff told me one day that the decision had been made to let me go. I was in church on a Sunday morning when the senior pastor told the thousands of people there that "drastic changes are coming in the church, and I will meet with all the youth and their parents on Tuesday night." I was sitting on the platform behind him thinking, *I know the drastic change. I'm getting fired tomorrow morning.*

That weekend was tough. My wife and I had one son, and she was pregnant with our second. She kept saying to me, "John, what are we going to do? Aren't you going to do something? Don't you need to make plans?"

I continually replied, "Honey, God sent us here, I've done nothing out of line, and I'm leaving the whole issue in God's hands."

11

The next morning I was asked to meet with the senior pastor in his office. This would be my first meeting with him in four months! The administrative pastor and another senior associate were supposed to join us. But when I walked into his office, the other two men were not there.

"You know, John, God sent you to this church, and you're not leaving until He is through with what He sent you for," the senior pastor told me. Then he looked at me and said, "Why does this administrator want to get rid of you so badly? Why does he want you fired?"

"I don't know!" I said. "I have no idea what I've done."

"Well, you need to find out what it is between you two and make things right. Will you please do that? I don't like this strife."

"Sure, Pastor, I will try, but I tell you, I don't know what it is." We talked a few more minutes, and before I left the senior pastor said that I could come see him anytime I liked.

About a month later I encountered some written evidence that revealed some improper things the administrative pastor was doing. I also learned that the man was trying to fire the music minister and another minister on staff. I thought to myself: *Okay, now it's time to show this document to the senior pastor. I want him to understand what this guy is up to. I will actually be doing the church a service, protecting the ministry.* I had concluded that the administrative pastor had so manipulated the senior pastor that he was blind to what was happening. I could fix that in short order. I felt almost noble about the possibility of exposing the man who was persecuting others and, of course, myself.

I made an appointment with the senior pastor, and the morning I was to see him, I set aside some time to pray. I struggled for forty minutes to pray effectively about the meeting. I kept asking the Lord, "How am I supposed to share this information with the senior pastor? Should I show him this piece of paper, or should I just tell him?" And I was getting no direction at all—zip. So I kept plowing ahead in prayer. Nothing happened. Finally I stopped, looked up, and cried out, "Lord, You don't want me to show this to him, do You?"

Something amazing happened immediately! The peace of God spread through me like a huge wave. It was pretty obvious to me what God wanted. I took the paper and ripped it into small pieces, throwing them in a waste can. *Either I'm the craziest man who's ever lived or I'm being very obedient to God,* I thought. Really, with all I had been through with this man who was after my hide, what I had just done did seem kind of nutty!

Another month went by. Nothing happened. I still had my job, but the air hadn't cleared. One morning I was praying outdoors in one of the church parking lots. I've always loved praying outside, and most days I went to the office about an hour and a half before church started or the offices opened up, so that I could spend some time alone with the Lord. As I was walking that morning, the administrative pastor drove up and pulled into his parking spot. Right then the Lord impressed on me very clearly: *I want you to go to him, apologize, and ask for his forgiveness.*

To be honest, I was pretty confused and upset. I said to the

Lord, "What? Me apologize to him? I haven't done anything to *him*. Lord, he's the one trying to get me fired. I already tore up that evidence! What do You mean that I need to apologize to him?"

I balked. Maybe I had not heard the Lord correctly. So I started praying about another topic real quick—missions. And instantly my prayer time became as dry as the Sahara Desert. It was as if God had vacated the area. Of course I knew He was still there; He's promised to never leave or forsake us. But His tangible presence had vanished. But sometimes I'm hardheaded, so I kept praying for the brothers and sisters in mission work.

I struggled on for about twenty more minutes before finally asking, "Okay, Lord, what are You saying to me right now?" And the Spirit of God came right back into my strolling prayer closet and spoke to me: "I want you to go to him and apologize."

I knew I was a goner. "I'm not going to get anywhere with You today, Lord, am I? I've got to go do this." So I got on the right track and started praying about what I needed to say to my boss because I didn't think I needed to apologize to him about anything. But the Lord showed me some things, so I went to my boss's office. I sat down across the desk from him and said, "I was out praying when you pulled up this morning. The Spirit of God spoke to me and said I needed to come to you and apologize because I've been very critical and judgmental of you. The Lord showed me how wrong this is. Will you please forgive me?"

The man looked surprised but said, "Well, sure. I forgive you." We talked a few more minutes, and that was it.

To be honest, I was still puzzled. But it did feel right to have obeyed.

Another six months went by, and during that time the administrative pastor's attacks subsided. I needed to go on a trip, and while I was out of town that weekend, everything fell apart for him. All of his wrongful actions were exposed—they were much worse than I was aware of. Some of his activities were even illegal, and he could have been charged and sent to jail. But the senior pastor decided to have mercy on him and not prosecute. The evidence was filed away at a lawyer's office, and the man was immediately fired.

The very pit the man was digging for me, he ended up falling into himself. Not only that, but I was vindicated before the pastor and office staff as they could see why the man did what he did against me. After being launched several months later from the church into a new ministry, I was asked to come back almost a dozen times to speak in the main services of the church.

Although I had known what Scripture said about how to respond to mistreatment, after this experience I really understood it deep in my heart. *I got it!* My life's not been the same since, and I'm eager now to share what I learned with you.

Do Not Avenge Yourselves

From the apostle Paul, in his letter to the Romans, we find some of the Bible's most explicit instructions on how to respond when mistreated.

Paul certainly knew all about the topic—from both sides of the coin. Before he had his dramatic conversion encounter with Jesus on the road to Damascus, Saul (Paul's name at that time) had persecuted every Christian he could get his hands on. Talk about a perpetrator of mistreatment! Saul was so full of anger and hatred against Christians that Scripture says, "He made havoc of the church, entering every house, and dragging off men and women, committing them to prison" (Acts 8:3). Saul was cheering the murdering mob on when Stephen was stoned and became a martyr. And on the very trip when God surrounded Saul with light and he fell to the ground, the Bible says he was "still breathing threats and murder against the disciples of the Lord" (Acts 9:1).

But it wasn't too long after Saul met Jesus that he learned himself what it feels like to be mistreated. After preaching his first great sermon and testifying so mightily that Jesus was in fact the Messiah, the Jews plotted to kill him. The only way he could get out of Damascus alive was to have some of the disciples lower him over the city wall in a basket. Later Saul (now called Paul) summarized the types of mistreatment he had received as an apostle of the gospel:

> From the Jews five times I received forty stripes minus one. Three times I was beaten with rods; once I was stoned; three times I was shipwrecked; a night and a day I have been in the deep; in journeys often, in perils of waters, in perils of robbers, in perils of my own countrymen, in perils of the Gentiles, in perils in the city, in

perils in the wilderness, in perils in the sea, in perils among false brethren; in weariness and toil, in sleeplessness often, in hunger and thirst, in fastings often, in cold and nakedness—besides the other things, what comes upon me daily: my deep concern for all the churches. (2 Corinthians 11:24–28)

Man, this guy could have written the book on mistreatment! And in a sense he did! Listen to what this well-qualified expert, inspired by the Holy Spirit, wrote on the topic:

Repay no one evil for evil. Have regard for good things in the sight of all men. If it is possible, as much as depends on you, live peaceably with all men. Beloved, do not avenge yourselves, but rather give place to wrath; for it is written, "Vengeance is Mine, I will repay," says the Lord. (Romans 12:17–19)

Did you catch that? Paul, after all the mistreatment he had received in serving the Lord Jesus Christ and His church, made the statement: "Repay no one evil for evil."

If I were reading these verses to you during one of my messages, I would urge you to say a loud "Amen!" to every line. Since I can't look you in the eye right now and make sure you are paying attention, I beg you to slow down and really grasp what God's Word is saying here. If you are a little drowsy, put the book down and go get a cup of coffee! If you want to successfully handle mistreatment, *you must get this!*

Paul is saying that our basic response when someone hurts us should not be concern about getting all of our rights and making sure we come out on top. In fact, whenever it's possible for us, we are to seek peace in our relationships with others.

Do you remember that old expression "Let it slide off you like water off a duck's back"? The idea is that we are to have an attitude of "taking things" instead of always fussing and fighting to make sure every wrong committed against us is made right.

Have you ever been around someone who just cannot let anything slide? If someone cuts in line at the supermarket checkout, this person always has to yell out, "Hey buddy! Can't you see there's a line here?" and then shoots the offender an angry look so full of acid it could strip the paint off a car.

That's not the response we are to have if we want to obey the command "Repay no one evil for evil."

And then Paul tells us why we don't need to be always looking out for ourselves: "Beloved, do not avenge yourselves . . . for it is written, 'Vengeance is Mine, I will repay,' says the Lord."

> **God isn't into small talk. He's into *big talk!* When He says something, He means it and says it with authority.**

There it is, the first important key to learning how to rise above all mistreatment—from the smallest slight to the biggest betrayal. By faith we understand and accept the idea that our heavenly Father promises to make things right on our behalf, if we commit it to Him. He is ultimately responsible to see justice done—not you or me.

These words of Scripture are not a suggestion or a recommendation; they are a command! When God speaks, He isn't like some people who can't stand silence and have to say something. God isn't into small talk. He's into *big talk!* When He says something, He means it and says it with authority.

Repeatedly in the Bible God says in so many words: "Don't think you are responsible for 'getting even' when you get hurt." Following are a few examples of what God has said on this topic:

- "Do not say, 'I will recompense evil'; wait for the LORD, and He will save you" (Prov. 20:22).

- "Vengeance is Mine, and recompense; their foot shall slip in due time; for the day of their calamity is at hand, and the things to come hasten upon them" (Deut. 32:35).

- "Do not say, 'I will do to him just as he has done to me; I [the Lord] will render to the man according to his work'" (Prov. 24:29).

- "For we know Him who said, 'Vengeance is Mine, I will repay,' says the Lord" (Heb. 10:30).

Are you seeing this? In the flesh we naturally do just the opposite—we often can't wait to get even. But that is wrong. God commands us to let Him bring about justice. It is an unrighteous thing for God's people to avenge themselves; it is a righteous thing for God to avenge His people.

God Will Avenge His People

This profound truth about not avenging ourselves is an example of how we Christians can get in trouble when we major on what God minors on, and minor on what He majors on. There are many topics in the Bible that are interesting and helpful but not major truths. Too often we spend too much time talking about these and yet never really get around to grappling with a big idea, like how God wants us to respond to the injustices we all receive.

I learned something as a young Christian that I'm grateful has never left me: It is really a slap in God's face, an insult to His character, when we act like we don't think He will do something that He's promised to do! It would be like me saying to one of my boys, "I'm going to give you a wonderful Christmas gift," but on a daily basis my son is saying, "Well, Dad, I know that you promised me a great gift, but I don't think you're going to do it!" What an insult to my integrity! That would hurt me and also make me angry.

How do you think God feels when we do this to Him? He says that after committing the injustice to Him, we are to "chill out" because He will avenge or make things right when we're mistreated. By our actions, do we show that we believe that is true?

That's why Jesus was so grieved every time people didn't believe that He would do what He said He was going to do.

Do you remember the time He told His disciples on the shore of Lake Galilee that they were going to get in the boat and sail to the other side? He didn't say, "Look, I hope we will make it across."

The time came to leave and everyone got in the boat. Jesus lay down to take a nap. He didn't need to stay up all night worrying that the boat might hit a rock and sink or that local pirates would commandeer the vessel and take them all hostage! Jesus spoke with authority because He was obedient to His Father in heaven. Jesus was just carrying out orders—"Take the boatload of disciples to the other side." So when the storm came up and the disciples went berserk with fear, the first thing Jesus did was to tell the storm to stop, then He turned around and rebuked the disciples for their lack of faith. He said in so many words, "I didn't tell you we were going to go halfway across this lake and sink. I said we were going to go to the other side."

God is good for His word. When He makes a promise, it's a "done deal." There are no flaws in His character. He cannot lie. He does not have bad days or occasional slumps. His word is rock solid. In the Bible, the Lord says, "I am the LORD, I do not change" (Mal. 3:6). The apostle James wrote that in God "there is no variation or shadow of turning" (James 1:17). We are told plainly that God will take care of righting the wrongs done to us. Our job is to trust what He has said and to obey.

There is one other point I want to make. Paul wrote that instead of avenging ourselves, we should "give place" or make room for wrath. In other words, we can actually mess up God's

> God is good for His word. When He makes a promise, it's a "done deal."

intent to take care of injustice. He means that by our wrong response to mistreatment, we actually hinder God's work in taking vengeance on our behalf. I will discuss this in greater detail later. For now it is enough for us to know that vengeance is not ours; it is His.

And that, my friend, is very good news. Just think of it— God Almighty takes note of what happens to each of us and promises, "I will take care of it."

Hallelujah!

3

The Right Way to Respond

We have learned that God wants us to let Him be in charge of dealing with our mistreatment. But just how are we to respond? The wrong way is to take things into our own hands. What is the right way?

Jesus' Example

If anyone knew how to handle mistreatment, it was our Lord Jesus Christ. When we observe how Jesus responded to tough situations in His life, then we'll truly understand how we should do it, too.

Jesus took quite a bit of abuse throughout His ministry. We sometimes forget this when we focus on all the wonderful things Jesus did—turning water into wine, healing the blind and lame, feeding thousands of people with a few crusts of bread and several fish, walking on water, chasing away demons, calming raging seas, raising the dead. That all seems glamorous and trouble-free. But we need to remember that Jesus' earthly life was much like our own—many days of fighting off attacks mixed in with the good days.

Jesus' mistreatment certainly began in a big way during His temptation in the wilderness where He was insulted and ridiculed by Satan. Then, as Jesus began His ministry, the criticism from people really kicked in. The religious leaders dogged His every step and continually harassed Him. His disciples did their best to follow and obey Him, but they often fell into disbelief and distrust. During His ministry a large contingent of His followers just packed it in and abandoned Him (see John 6:66). Even His own brothers and sisters did not believe in Him and thought He was mentally disturbed and tried to get Him to come home and stop embarrassing the family (see Mark 3:21).

But the worst abuse and mistreatment came near the end. In the final days before His death, Jesus powerfully demonstrated how we are to respond when we are mistreated.

Of course we remember how each disciple, one by one, turned his back on Jesus. It started with Judas's decision to trade the Son of God for some easy cash. But the other disciples could not even stay awake to pray with Jesus, and the Bible says they all ran away (see Mark 14:50). Then one of His closest friends, Peter, actually cursed angrily and denied that he knew Him.

But the worst treatment was still to come. Next Jesus had to endure His sham trial. Jesus modeled for us, at the very end of His ordeal, how to respond when we are mistreated:

> Immediately, in the morning, the chief priests held a consultation with the elders and scribes and the whole council; and they bound Jesus, led Him away, and delivered Him to Pilate. Then

Pilate asked Him, "Are You the King of the Jews?" He answered and said to him, "It is as you say." And the chief priests accused Him of many things, but He answered nothing. Then Pilate asked Him again, saying, "Do You answer nothing? See how many things they testify against You!" But Jesus still answered nothing, so that Pilate marveled. (Mark 15:1–5)

Did you note what this Scripture says about how Jesus responded? After basically just giving His name, rank, and serial number—what our American soldiers are told to do if they become prisoners of war—Jesus "answered nothing." This is really incredible! If anyone in the history of the world ever had reasons to "stand up for himself" and make sure the judge knew what a raw deal he had received, it was Jesus.

This was a court of law—the highest in the land—and the witnesses (the chief priests) against Jesus were telling lies about Him. It's important to understand that the chief priests were not only religious leaders, but political leaders as well. Whenever Rome conquered a territory or nation, the captive land was allowed to rule itself under

> **If anyone in the history of the world ever had reasons to "stand up for himself" and make sure the judge knew what a raw deal he had received, it was Jesus.**

Rome's supervision. So, when the chief priests appeared in this courtroom, they were the most influential citizens of the entire nation. And what these guys said about Jesus did not contain an ounce of truth. Still, Jesus didn't answer them with one word. He did not defend Himself!

Why did He choose to remain silent and not defend Himself? Because He had committed Himself and His case obediently to the One who would judge righteously—His Father in heaven.

And Pilate, who was in charge of this whole railroad of injustice, knew what was happening—to such an extent that he finally blurted out, "Why are You not defending Yourself against these lies?" When Jesus still didn't answer, Pilate "marveled." There was no question in Pilate's mind that Jesus was being framed out of envy and that His accusers had no case. Pilate had never seen anything like this before. Men coming to his court were normally very eager to make a defense. The possibility of punishment, imprisonment, or even execution by the Romans was not a pleasant prospect.

Historical records from this time period show that Pilate knew about Jesus before He came into the courtroom. Like Herod, Pilate was intrigued by Jesus. There is some evidence that Pilate actually at one point had a conversation with Jesus. Pilate's wife even had reported having a dream about Jesus and told her husband, "Have nothing to do with this man, He's just" (see Matt. 27:19). Then, during the Crucifixion, it was Pilate who created the sign for the cross—"The King of the Jews." The chief priests vigorously complained to Pilate that it was Jesus who had made this claim and the sign should be removed. But Pilate would not do it and said, "What I have written, I have written" (John 19:22).

So there Pilate was, looking at Jesus, and listening to these bloodthirsty liars who wanted Jesus executed on trumped-up charges. And Jesus didn't answer a word because He had committed His case into the hands of His Father, who would judge it rightly.

This is the personal example Jesus left us.

So it comes as no surprise that the apostle Paul also emphasized this idea. In fact, both Jesus and Paul were very good students of the Jewish Scriptures and essentially quoted verbatim what Solomon had written hundreds of years earlier:

> If your enemy is hungry, give him bread to eat;
> And if he is thirsty, give him water to drink;
> For so you will heap coals of fire on his head,
> And the LORD will reward you. (Proverbs 25:21–22)

The lesson for us is that when we would like to get even with anyone for hurting or mistreating us in some way, we need to reach out—not to punch his lights out!—but to hand him a piece of bread or a cool can of soda pop. Of course this will feel unnatural, and acts of kindness like these often require quite a bit of creativity. But to be obedient to God's plan, we must bless those who have made our lives miserable.

So if someone has just ruffled your feathers or committed the most grievous betrayal—or any hurtful action in between—the basic response is the same:

- If he's thirsty, make a pitcher of iced tea.
- If she's hungry, fire up the barbecue.
- If he's broke, write out a check.
- If she's lonely, give her a call.
- If he's had an affair, continue to work on the marriage.
- If she cuts you off in traffic, smile and drive on.
- If he's given you grief, work overtime for him for free.

And if showing such kindness to people who have dragged you and your feelings through the mud makes you feel uncomfortable or even taken advantage of, remember what Jesus went through for you.

In His instructions to His disciples, which apply to you and me, too, Jesus explained why, if we follow Him, we are not to defend ourselves if we are unjustly accused. Think of it this way: When you try so hard to prove your innocence, you quickly put yourself at the mercy of your accuser. For this reason, Jesus said:

Agree with your adversary quickly, while you are on the way with him, lest your adversary deliver you to the judge, the judge hand you over to the officer, and you be thrown into prison. Assuredly, I say to you, you will by no means get out of there till you have paid the last penny. (Matthew 5:25–26)

In other words, your accuser will get out of you everything he believes you owe him.

The moment you start making a stink and seeking to justify and defend yourself, you make the person accusing you your judge. Because when you try to answer and defend all of his charges, you in a sense are now

> **When you try so hard to prove your innocence, you quickly put yourself at the mercy of your accuser.**

submitted to him and his view of things. He is calling the shots. If he's not your judge, why do you need to answer to him? You elevate him as your judge when you feel you have to defend yourself.

By rising up and trying to defend yourself at all costs, you forfeit your spiritual right of protection. In the process your accuser rises above you, as his influence is elevated by your self-defense. You actually give him greater influence over you by trying so hard to stand up for your rights!

A Personal Example

Let me give an example to illustrate this: Some years ago an influential person in Christian circles made a false statement about me to two large organizations. There wasn't an ounce of truth in what he said, but in just a matter of days the accusation cost our ministry $10,000.

I found out what had happened in a phone call from our ministry's administrator. It made me mad. Honestly, I was ready to hit the ceiling. When I received the call I was sitting in an airline lounge about to leave on an international flight to Sweden. That was the Lord's kindness to me. Because of where I was, I really couldn't do anything—but calm down and pray. I've learned something over the years: when you get in a crisis or situation where you have been mistreated, don't do anything until you sleep on it. If you are not hearing from God while you are awake, He'll talk to you during your sleep.

So I boarded that international flight, and I was steaming. In my flesh I struggled, pondering numerous ways I could make things "right" doing it my way. But then I fell asleep somewhere over the Atlantic Ocean.

The next morning when I woke up as we started our descent into Stockholm, the thought hit me—*You can see this as a theft. You can demand in the Spirit that the thief must restore seven times* (see Prov. 6:31). But that thought wasn't especially satisfying. I still was holding resentment. Then I had another thought: *Or, you can not see this as a loss of funds, but rather as a gift!* This actually felt much better to me. The sting went out of my emotions. I started feeling happy—it's fun to give! And besides, when you give a gift, the Lord promises a hundredfold return (see Mark 10:29–30).

I began praying about this second option, and when I returned to America I ran the idea by both Lisa and my pastor, Ted Haggard. Both of them liked the idea, too. So to seal the deal with the Lord, Lisa and I got together and prayed, "Father, this money we've lost because of what the man said, we just give it as a gift in Jesus' name; we bless these funds in the name of Jesus."

That finally did it for me. My anger was gone. I was happy. I could forgive and move on. The whole matter was in the Father's capable hands.

Ten days later, a couple rang the doorbell at our home in Colorado. They were from Texas, so it wasn't as if they just happened to be in our neighborhood. I opened the door, and they handed me an envelope, talked for ten minutes, and left. Inside the envelope were a card and a check made out to our ministry for $10,000. I immediately said to Lisa, "Look at this, Honey! There's onefold—ninety-nine to go!"

Jesus was so adamant about this issue that He commanded us to go above and beyond the minimum in blessing our enemies or adversaries. He said that in choosing to not resist an evil person, we should not just avoid defending ourselves but we should dig deep in handing out kindness and blessings to the person who has mistreated us.

One illustration Jesus used was: "Whoever compels you to go one mile, go with him two" (Matt. 5:41). When Jesus was on earth, the Roman occupiers could ask any person who was not a Roman citizen to carry equipment for a mile. What Jesus really meant was, "Get rid of this slave mentality and become a servant." A slave does the minimum requirement. A servant performs to the maximum potential. A slave *has* to; the servant *gets* to. A slave is stolen from; the servant gives.

Coals of Fire

Now what did Solomon (and later Paul) mean by saying we will pour "heaping coals of fire" on the heads of people who have offended us? That doesn't sound very spiritual!

The essential meaning is that when you do not defend yourself but actually reach out in kindness to someone who has mistreated you, in most instances the person will feel ashamed and will back off from making further accusations or mistreating you even more. The perpetrator will have a "burning sense of shame" that more than likely will end the matter—and perhaps prepare the way for repentance, reconciliation, and even friendship.

So the first reason God tells us to not defend ourselves or to take vengeance on our enemy is because it makes room for His righteous judgment and keeps our hearts right.

In case you are thinking that being obedient is just for your benefit and the ultimate good of the person who mistreats you—which of course is true—there is a greater purpose. Paul summed up his point here by saying, "Do not be overcome by evil but overcome evil with good."

Even coming from the apostle Paul, this is a huge serving of the truth! What he was saying is that by responding in the way God wants us to when we are mistreated, we become His dynamic

THE RIGHT WAY TO RESPOND

agents in overcoming evil. Our good works are not just "nice" and effective in making our relationships work better—of course there's nothing wrong with that. Our world needs plenty of such salt and light! But the greater implication of what Paul taught here is that the obedient Christian, following humbly the example of Jesus, who did not seek to defend Himself when mistreated, joins the ranks of the finest warriors in advancing the cause of Christ and the kingdom of God in defeating evil!

Praise God—what an honor that is! And it all starts with turning the other cheek and staying quiet—letting God be our defender when life isn't fair.

4

The Issue of Authority

Often the mistreatment people receive comes in some way from someone who is in authority over them. In the family it may involve a father's or mother's overly harsh treatment of a child. Sometimes teachers or coaches misuse their authority to shame a student who's "just not getting it" or an athlete who can't catch any ball thrown his way. Bosses may unfairly blame employees for shipping mistakes in a warehouse or the loss of a big sale to a competitor. Occasionally police officers are falsely accused of discriminating against people of certain racial or ethnic groups. And perhaps most sadly there are even cases where people in authority in churches misuse their power over others to bully people or get what they want.

Governing Authorities Are Appointed by God

So what does the Bible say about how we should respond to authority? Once again the apostle Paul made a clear statement on the topic: "Let every soul be subject to the governing authorities" (Rom. 13:1).

Even the most independent, free-spirited American has a hard time wiggling out of the meaning of that verse. The phrase "every soul" just does not allow for exceptions. And "be subject to the governing authorities" is equally pointed and clear. We need to swallow our independent inclinations and step up the truth of this: We Christians are not to resist the legitimate authority in our lives. (Below, I will discuss the very few situations where it is necessary for a follower of Christ to disobey authority.)

It took a while to accept this in all areas of my life. I still don't always get it right, but the Word of God has changed me, and I'm doing much better than I used to. In the past, for example, if I was on the highway and suddenly saw some red and blue lights flashing in my rearview mirror, I might have tried to "bind the devil" and pray my way out of a ticket. However, I don't think that's the response the apostle Paul was looking for when he said, "Be subject to the governing authorities."

> We need to swallow our independent inclinations and step up the truth of this: We Christians are not to resist the legitimate authority in our lives.

The last time I was pulled over (I'm pleased to say it seldom occurs anymore—my right foot has lost some weight!), one of my employees was riding in the car with me. This young man was raised by a father who just despised policemen. So when he saw the flashing lights behind us, my rider got hot under the collar and started complaining about the cop. Right away I said, "Why are you saying these things? Don't blame this policeman! He is a servant given by God to protect the public. I was speeding! He's just doing his job."

The policeman came to my window and collected my license and car registration. He walked back to his car to check me out on his computer. None of us like this part. It's embarrassing to be sitting beside the road, with other drivers slowing to get a good look as they roll by.

In a few minutes the patrolman tapped on my window. "Mr. Bevere," he said, "because of the speed you were traveling, I'm going to have to give you a ticket." At this point I could almost feel the officer's skin tighten, preparing for some kind of angry response from me. But all I said was, "Sir, I want to thank you for what you did. I was wrong. I'm guilty; I will not show up in court to defend myself. I deserve this, and I want to thank you for your service to our community because we need you. God bless you."

I've learned to wait until the officer actually gives me the ticket because after he hands it to you, he can't take it back. I do this because most officers are so stunned they look like they want to say, "Can I have that back?" But it's too late.

My staff member in the car was taken aback by my behavior and learned a life lesson. He saw in action the way we are commanded to respond to those in authority over us—no back talk, no blaming others, no huffing and puffing. We are to accept respectfully what we deserve.

The main reason we do this is because God is so clear about the matter. Reading on in Romans 13:1:

> For there is no authority except from God, and the authorities that exist are appointed by God.

In the day we live in, authority has a negative reputation, maybe even more so in our Western culture than in other parts of the world. I think it is fair to say that the seeds of rebellion were sown in the 1930s, when professors in our universities began to indoctrinate students in the liberalism and rationalism imported from Europe. The fruits of this became apparent during the 1960s, reflected in bad attitudes against authority. The protests against the war in Vietnam, the breaking down of traditional sexual morality, the rise of the drug culture, the increasing divorce rate, the decaying of values seen in movies and television, and riots in the inner cities—these and so many other shifts all were linked in some way to the declining respect for authority. Students, who were protesting and running wild on campuses, called policemen "pigs." Respect for government leaders fell because of controversy over the war and foreign policy. Watergate was the first of many scandals. A kind of tabloid fever infected much of the news media; so many of our heroes and others in public life or positions of authority had their reputations dragged through the mud.

And then probably worst of all, several prominent leaders in the church were caught in sexual affairs or stealing or mismanaging the Lord's money in their ministries. No wonder respect for authority seemed like naive foolishness. As a society we are now reaping the harvest of those seeds which were cleverly sown in our society by the enemy.

The only problem with any disregard for authority—and it is a big problem—is that God says we are to respect legitimate authority no matter what because "all authority" comes from God. Even more pointedly, all authority is *appointed* by God. Let that sink in—there is *no authority not appointed by God!*

There may be an occasional situation where authority must be disobeyed, and there is such a thing as illegitimate authority. I will discuss these issues later. But those really are quite rare exceptions, and the Scripture is clear that every person is to be "subject to the governing authorities."

Many people really struggle with the meaning of this. It can seem that this commandment is so lofty as to be virtually impossible for any Christian to obey. But that is the challenge of being a follower of Christ! None of us can do what He commands unless we surrender in our flesh and allow God to fill us with His grace. The Christian life runs on supernatural power. Without that power every one of us is "toast."

Something I'm very thankful for is that right after I met and received Jesus Christ as my Savior at my fraternity at Purdue University, I decided that if the Bible was the Word of God, then I was going to believe and obey it, whether or not I understood everything I read. I did this not because I already was such a great Christian, but primarily because of my fear of God. I knew I had been rescued from my sin and my future in hell. I did not think it was wise to sort the Scriptures and decide which ones applied to my life and which ones didn't. Of course there have been times because of ignorance that I've acted contrary to Scripture, but to the extent I have just simply obeyed God's revealed Word, I have been protected from evil and abundantly blessed.

All legitimate authority comes from God! Although people are often appointed or elected to important positions where they can rule others, they are in those positions of authority because God put them there.

I remember when this became very clear to me. Back in 1992, after Bill Clinton was elected to his first term, I was depressed for several days. To be honest, I was very disappointed that this man was going to be president of the United States. Around my third day of moping about this, God told me in so many words, "John, nobody gets into office without My knowing about it." He reminded me of what Scripture says—that everyone in authority is "appointed." Even though we may live in a nation where we vote for and elect our leaders, all of them ultimately are in office through divine appointment.

You must let this truth sink deeply into your mind and spirit: All of the legitimate authority figures in your life—a parent, a boss, a teacher, a pastor, a judge, a congressman—have been appointed by God!

Ungodly Authorities

It's at this point where some high walls of resistance often go up. You might be thinking: *But what about people in authority who are downright evil, mean, and harsh? Did God appoint them? Was Adolf Hitler selected by God? You cannot be telling me that all authority is appointed by God, because I have heard of or experienced some downright bad authority!*

We have a clear choice to make: *Do we trust the Bible?* If our answer is "Yes," then we must accept and obey what it says about authority. God appoints people to their positions of authority. However, He is not responsible for how the men and women in authority act. Many of them are mean and abusive. We have to separate authority itself from how that authority is used. The appointment is from God; the bad qualities and evil behavior are provided by human beings. So it is safe to say it like this: All authority is from God, but not all authorities are godly.

It is very interesting to observe how the apostle Paul arranged his instruction on how we are to respond when mistreated by authority figures. First he reminds us that we are not to take vengeance, and then in his very next point Paul discusses authority. I think the Holy Spirit inspired it this way because He knew, as well as Paul knew—from personal experience—that there would always be people in positions of authority who would take advantage of, mistreat, and abuse those under their control. Paul had to make crystal clear for us what God says repeatedly: "Vengeance is Mine, I will repay."

In his writing Peter also elaborated on the same subject:

Honor all people. Love the brotherhood. Fear God. Honor the king. Servants, be submissive to your masters with all fear, not only to the good and gentle, but also to the harsh. (1 Peter 2:17–18)

In effect what Peter said is: "How do you think you can honor God, whom you've *not* seen, when you can't even honor the person He's placed in authority over you, whom you *do* see?"

During this period of time, when slavery was common, many of the believers themselves were servants. Although slavery always is repugnant, in some ways being a slave or servant in New Testament days was like being an employee today. In fact some slaves were highly educated—doctors, librarians, teachers, musicians, and secretaries were among them. Some were obviously superior to their masters (Source: *Interpreter's Commentary on the Whole Bible*). But the instruction Peter gave was to "do what the boss says."

An interesting fact is that the king Peter told his readers to honor was Herod Agrippa I, the same king who was cruelly persecuting and executing believers. Peter wasn't asking his Christian brothers and sisters to submit to the authority of a "nice, good king." He was asking them to obey a vicious despot who wanted their heads. The only way they could do that was to see beyond the king's personality, decisions, and actions, and recognize the authority given him by God.

Frankly, there are some things we believers choose to do obediently that we probably would not do if we didn't fear God. In human terms it doesn't make a lot of sense to subject yourself to a cruel king. But it always makes perfect sense to obey God.

The Fear of the Lord

Today we don't hear too much preaching or teaching about the fear of the Lord. That's unfortunate, because an appropriate fear of God is a very healthy quality for any person to possess. Centuries before Jesus appeared on earth as the incarnate Son of God, Isaiah prophesied that Jesus would have this quality:

> His delight is in the *fear of the LORD*, and He shall not judge by the sight of His eyes, nor decide by the hearing of His ears; but with righteousness He shall judge the poor, and decide with equity for the meek of the earth. (Isaiah 11:3–4, emphasis added)

You must understand that the only way any of us will ever be able to always submit to authority—in addition to walking in the power of the Holy Spirit—is to have a proper fear of the Lord. We will then refrain from judging the leader's personality, but see the authority God has placed on the leader.

It's really sad, but in America we often say to our leaders, "You will have to earn my respect." Instead of that, a person who fears God will say, "You have my respect already, because I recognize the authority God has given you." The believer says this knowing full well that God looks at the heart and does not judge by the words or actions of a person's life. His evaluation or judgment is based on a man's or woman's motivations and is always righteous.

The same instructions on authority are in place for us. God

hasn't changed His mind on this topic. Only when we fear the Lord—when we have such a reverent respect for God that we would not even consider questioning what He asks us to do—will we obediently accept that all authority on the earth has one Source—God.

Elaborating on the apostle Paul's teaching, Peter insisted, "Servants, be submissive to your masters." In our day, for the word *servants* you could substitute *employees, students, church members, enlisted personnel, officers*—let's face it, everyone has someone in authority over them. Even the most powerful person on earth, the president of the United States, must submit to the authority of the United States Constitution and the laws of the land. And of course, ultimately the president answers to God, who appointed him to office! Peter's instruction applies to everyone.

> Let's face it, everyone has someone in authority over them.

The attitude we are to have is "submission with fear no matter what the authority figure is like"—in Peter's words—"not only to the good and gentle, but also to the harsh."

Thankfully, most of the time you and I have at least one person in authority over us who is a really nice man or woman. It's not that difficult to accept and obey leadership from that kind of person. At our home church in Colorado, Pastor Ted Haggard is a good and gentle shepherd of his flock. It's a joy to submit to his authority and leadership. But Peter didn't stop with the nice guys in authority. He specifically pointed out that we are to submit to the "bad guys," too.

Long ago, when I was still grappling with the meaning of Peter's words in this verse, I thought I might find some kind of "loophole" if I looked at the meaning of the original Greek word *harsh*. I wondered if the Bible translators had gotten a bit carried away with their English interpretation. Had there been a mistake? Did Peter really mean "harsh"? I checked the books of several Greek scholars, starting with *Thayers Greek Dictionary*. His meaning for the word *skolios*, which is Greek for "harsh," is "crooked, perverse, wicked, and unfair."

That wasn't quite what I was hoping for, so next I took a look at the meaning in *Vine's Expository Dictionary*: "tyrannical or unjust leaders." I kept looking in books by other scholars and came up with more words that essentially meant "harsh, dishonest, cruel, unreasonable."

I admit that this is one biblical truth that does not go down real easy. Everything in the way we look at life in the flesh shouts that this is wrong—why in the world should we submit ourselves to a cruel, unreasonable, unjust, and dishonest tyrant? The reason, even if it makes us squirm, is that God *tells* us to do this. But we must never forget that He is a wonderful Father, the best Daddy in the universe. So we can know with confidence that obeying authority as He commands is good for us.

Should We Ever Disobey Authority?

Are there times when we have a legitimate right not to submit to authority? Yes, although such circumstances are rare. For example, occasionally in our lives we run into an illegitimate authority established by cultic leaders or others who find a way to appoint themselves to positions of power and sneer at God and His ways. Paul said we don't need to give them even an hour of submission (see Gal. 2:4–5). To put it in more modern terms, he was saying, "We don't give them a New York minute!"

But there is a basic rule to remember if you think you've encountered a time the Bible would permit you to disobey someone in authority. The guideline is as follows: *When authority commands us to do something that clearly contradicts Scripture, we need to draw the line and respectfully say "No."*

A great scriptural example of disobedience to authority occurred in the story of Shadrack, Meshach, and Abed-Nego (Dan. 3:8–30). These three young men, with Daniel, were hauled away to Babylon under the leadership of King Nebuchadnezzar. These young men, along with the rest of the realm, were ordered to bow down to the idol of the king every time they heard the musical instruments playing. For the Jews, that directive was a clear violation of the second commandment—"You shall have no other gods before Me" (Deut. 5:7). So when the musical instruments played, these three brave boys did not bow. When King Nebuchadnezzar heard about it, he was furious. They were brought before him, but they came respectfully. They didn't sneer and say, "You pagan jerk, we're not going to obey you!" They looked at him and said, "Your majesty, we will not obey" (see Dan. 3:16–18 NLT). They honored him and the authority given him by God. But they refused to dishonor the Source of authority, God Almighty, and did not obey their king's command to sin.

David also demonstrated how to react to an illegitimate use of authority. When Saul was doing all he could to catch David and make him a wall-hanging, David did not stay at the palace. He fled to the wilderness, but he never surrendered his attitude of submission and respect for the king God had placed in authority over him.

One of the more difficult situations today is when authority is being misused between a husband and wife. As the Bible teaches, the husband has been placed in authority over his wife and children. If the husband misuses his authority, the wife—with the same attitude used by David with Saul—may need to resist respectfully and perhaps remove herself from a husband who is out of control. It is important to realize that there is a difference between submission and obedience. The wife, by having a respectful attitude, can still submit, but she does not have to obey a husband who is abusing her by asking her to do things that go against God's Word.

Because of confusion on this issue, sometimes women end up in unhealthy and dangerous situations because a husband is physically abusing them or their children and they're saying, "Well, I have to stay obedient to my husband." No, they don't. That is an example of where authority can be respectfully but firmly resisted.

She has the right, perhaps even the responsibility, to ask him to depart and send him home to Mama. If he doesn't leave, she should leave, but as with David, maintain the respect for his authority.

> **The Bible does not teach unconditional obedience to authority; it does teach unconditional submission.**

The Bible does not teach unconditional obedience to authority; it does teach unconditional submission. There's a difference. Obedience deals with our actions, whereas submission deals with our hearts.

Peter wrote that it is the submission of the wife that is going to win her husband when he sees her "chaste conduct" and "gentle and quiet spirit" (1 Peter 3:2, 4). His point was that if a husband is not obeying the Word, here's the way his wife will be used by God to speed up a change in his heart and behavior.

I know that these truths are often difficult to comprehend. What is God up to? Why is He so insistent on these topics? Is there more to this than meets the eye? Of course! His plans and intentions will be our focus in the chapters that follow.

5

The Role of Suffering

If you have been a Christian for even a short time, you already know that God really loves His children. One of the most hideous lies of Satan is when he whispers to us that "God is really an old grump and kind of mean. You better keep your distance from Him, because He's just waiting for you to goof up so He can punish you."

No, no—a thousand times no! Our Abba Father God is a wonderful Daddy, the best in the universe! He will never do anything that conflicts with His character. He does not tell us to do things like "do not return evil for evil" because He wants to make us miserable. He does that because He loves us. And on top of it, He has wonderful blessings planned for us when we obey. Such is the case when we hold our tongues and refrain from striking back when we are mistreated.

Let's go a bit further in the passage we are examining in 1 Peter. In the last chapter we discussed how God wants us to submit to those in authority over us—whether they are nice or harsh. This is what Peter tells us next:

> For this is commendable, if because of conscience toward God
> one endures grief, suffering wrongfully. (1 Peter 2:19)

Here we get an interesting insight into one of the things that pleases God. When someone mistreats us and we endure gracefully the suffering and grief that come as a result, God likes it. He finds this "commendable" or worthy of approval and praise. Now don't be mistaken: God is not sadistic; He's not up in heaven jumping up and down with joy that you or I have had to endure some unfairness. No, He aches with us just as He ached when Jesus had to suffer unfairly. When Peter said that we do this "because of conscience toward God," he meant that God loves it when we are so sensitive and obedient to His wishes that we will even endure suffering in the process.

So the next time you find yourself enduring some difficult things because someone in authority over you is not exercising power and control in a way that honors God, just say to yourself: "I know God does not like it that this person or institution is mistreating me. But He loves the fact that I am taking it with a respectful, submissive attitude. God is pleased with me! So I'm going to commit the outcome to Him."

When that happens, instead of moaning and groaning about how hard life is, just give yourself a huge pat on the back.

Peter then went on to explain more specifically the situations where God really appreciates patient suffering on His behalf:

For what credit is it if, when you are beaten for your faults, you take it patiently? But when you do good and suffer, if you take it patiently, this is commendable before God. (1 Peter 2:20)

In other words, if we do something wrong and get punished for it, we should not label that "persecution." That's just life! If we do something stupid or illegal, we should not spiritualize the consequences. Being punished for doing what is clearly wrong is called "self-inflicted persecution." God has set up earthly authorities to discipline and correct us in such instances.

> If we do something wrong and get punished for it, we should not label that "persecution." That's just life!

If, on your tax return, you claim to have six children but really only have three, when the IRS investigates and confronts you with the truth—and you owe a ton of back taxes plus interest—don't go to your Bible study group and ask for prayer to get relief from the government's persecution! Or even more ridiculous, don't predict to your friends that God is planning a great reward for you because of the persecution you are suffering on His behalf. Just admit your guilt, pay the money, repent, and don't ever do that again.

There's a way I can guarantee you will never have to face self-inflicted persecution: just do what's right! Much of the Christian life involves such common sense.

What Peter really was referring to here is legitimate or "righteous" persecution. That's when you're doing what is right, but you still end up getting blamed for something that's not your fault. That's obviously "unfair treatment."

Now here's a truth I want you never to forget: When you get treated unfairly, instead of moaning, whining, complaining, or groaning, get out of your chair, lift your hands, shout for joy, and do a little jig. You have done something God likes, and He has a reward for you that is well worth that kind of response. I'll have more to say on this later!

The Calling of Every Believer

One of the questions that people frequently ask me is "How can I know my calling?" Of course they usually mean by that: "What is the particular ministry God has in mind for me?"

Now unless I know the person very well or the Holy Spirit has given me some particular insight, I don't know how to answer that question—*specifically*. But there is *one* answer I can always give that is 100 percent right for every believer: Your calling is *to handle unfair treatment correctly.*

Often I get a very subdued, unenthusiastic response to that statement! Most of us have something a little more glamorous in mind for "our calling." And for sure there are other things we are called to do for the Lord Jesus and the advance of the kingdom of God. But it is also true that every one of us is called to suffer. The Bible is crystal clear on this point. Here's how Peter put it:

For to this you were called, because Christ also suffered for us, leaving us an example, that you should follow His steps. (1 Peter 2:21)

The *Amplified Bible* makes the meaning even more straightforward: "For even to this were you called [it is inseparable from your vocation]. For Christ also suffered for you, leaving you [His personal] example, so that you should follow in His footsteps."

> **If you align yourself with Christ, a part of your job description is suffering—just as He did for you.**

Did you catch that phrase "inseparable from your vocation"? That means that no matter what you do for God, you must accept the fact that suffering unfair treatment will be interwoven with it. If you align yourself with Christ, a part of your job description is suffering—just as He did for you.

Since we now know what is expected of us, just what did Jesus do that we are to imitate? What was His personal example? Peter gives us the answer, saying this about our Lord:

"Who committed no sin, nor was deceit found in His mouth"; who, when He was reviled, did not revile in return; when He suffered, He did not threaten, but committed Himself to Him who judges righteously. (1 Peter 2:22–23)

As we learned earlier, even though Jesus was perfect, He still was accused wrongfully of many things. Yet He never got defensive or tried to convince anyone that He was a victim. When people reviled or insulted Him, He took it graciously. He refused to get into any kind of "tit-for-tat" games. He did not fight back with digs, trash talk, or snappy put-downs. He never returned evil for evil. And even though He was the Son of God, don't you think that in His humanity He had an urge to stand up for Himself now and then? Sometimes He did engage in debate with the Pharisees and other religious leaders, but you won't find Jesus ever going on the attack to defend His "rights." Why was Jesus able to take so much mistreatment and abuse and not fight back?

There's a little phrase here in Peter's letter that explains everything—and also gives us the precise reason why we should not slash back when mistreated. Peter says of Jesus that He "committed Himself to Him who judges righteously."

That's it! Jesus knew that His Father was in control of His life and all the events that might happen to Him. He was acquainted intimately with His heavenly Father. There was no doubt in His mind that God Almighty would right all wrongs in His timing. Jesus didn't have to fight for His own rights. And neither do we. The awesome Ruler of the universe is not sleeping and unaware of what's going on when the righteous suffer on His behalf.

I will never forget a time when I was being attacked by a person of authority in my life. Accusations were being brought against me that just weren't true, and I regret to say, I was frantically defending myself for months.

While all of this was happening, one day I was in prayer and the Holy Spirit spoke to me. "Son," He said, "as long as you defend yourself, this is what I'm doing." And then I saw a vision of the Lord where He was visible to me only from His shoulders down. I could not see His face, and what stood out to me was that His hands and arms were securely restrained behind His back.

As I prayed, He impressed on me: "Now the moment you stop defending yourself, this is what will happen." Then I saw those arms and hands no longer withheld; rather the Holy Spirit was actively involved in the case others were bringing against me.

That definitely is a picture of what God will do for you and me when we obey His commandment and embrace our calling to suffer mistreatment correctly on His behalf. We stop fighting our own battles and by our words and actions say, "I belong to the God of the universe. He keeps His word. He's a great Daddy. I'll let Him take care of me. Justice will be done in God's timing. He will make sure that I am treated fairly. I will not return evil for evil. All I have to do is commit this to Him."

Once you become genuinely His, there is no unjust suffering

> Any unjust suffering you go through will result in a blessing down the line—if you respond God's way.

you will ever live through that doesn't have a reason behind it. God will not permit it. Any unjust suffering you go through will result in a blessing down the line—if you respond God's way.

The man or woman who walks that path will see the mighty hand of God executing righteous judgment.

The Ministry of Mistreatment

There is a result—when we handle mistreatment correctly—that may just blow your gaskets! Are you ready to hear this? You will love it!

To explain this, I first need to set the stage by sharing a verse from Hebrews:

> By faith Noah, being divinely warned of things not yet seen, moved with godly fear, prepared an ark for the saving of his household, by which *he condemned the world* and became heir of the righteousness which is according to faith. (Hebrews 11:7, emphasis added)

Notice this verse does not say, "God condemned the world." There is quite a powerful truth in this verse. It says that Noah, by being obedient, brought on the condemnation of the world. Wow! This is the power unleashed when we believers just do what God asks. Pay careful attention to this: God doesn't suggest or recommend. He commands us to not avenge ourselves when we are mistreated. Why? Because in so doing we "heap coals of fire on the head" of the one who is mistreating us. And the result is the speeding up of God's judgment.

When we hear the word *judgment,* too often the image that comes to mind is hellfire and brimstone. But judgment in the New Testament really means "a decision of God for or against." Do you know what the decision of God might be in a particular situation? Consider this: That person who is mistreating you may be forgiven of sin, saved, and delivered from his behavior!

I know a woman whose husband mistreated her for years. This husband just would not allow God into his life. His wife tried as hard as she could to manipulate him into accepting Christ and becoming a godly man. But he just would not do it.

Finally, after she had struggled in frustration for years, one day the Lord said to her, "How long will you continue to hinder your husband's salvation?"

"What did You say?" she asked.

Then the Lord showed her all the things she was doing and saying that actually messed up and slowed down God's working in her husband's life. The Lord asked her to stop doing those things, and she finally obeyed. She became quiet and much more supportive. She did not whine and criticize. She stood back and let God do His thing.

Two months later her husband was saved! Since then I've been a guest in their home, and, believe me, her husband is a new creation in Christ. She doesn't have to nag him anymore to be a man of God. By her obedience this wife actually sped up God's judgment or decision to intervene.

This example is just one illustration in what I would call the "ministry of mistreatment." God always has a reason for what He asks us to do. When He commands us to turn away from revenge and let Him execute judgment, it's not just some pet idea of God's that somehow makes Him feel good or important. No, God doesn't waste His energy or resources. He has a purpose for the suffering we endure while mistreated.

But just how does it come about? And when?

Let's continue to find the answers in God's Word.

6

Blessed Are the Mistreated

Do you enjoy being blessed?

That may seem like kind of a ridiculous question, but I've run into some Christians who almost act like they are *more* favored by God if they do not grab hold of and receive many of His magnificent promises!

I have always thought that Jesus must have run into something of the same attitude because of the way He questioned the crippled man who was lying by the Bethesda pool. Jesus said to him, "Do you want to be made well?" (John 5:6). Doesn't that seem like an odd question—unless there were some people Jesus was encountering who really didn't want what He had to offer?

As I have hinted at earlier in this book, God doesn't ask us to "not return evil for evil" when mistreated without offering us a significant blessing in return. Of course we should never act like disgruntled employees when dealing with Father God. He requires our obedience, and we should give it joyfully because we are His precious children. But our Father in heaven is a huge

Giver, and He wants to bless us for bearing mistreatment and suffering on His behalf.

Here's how the apostle Peter described what will happen:

> Not returning evil for evil or reviling for reviling, but on the contrary blessing, knowing that you were called to this, *that you may inherit a blessing.* (1 Peter 3:9, emphasis added)

Those of us who preach and minister to the body of Christ can get in trouble when we shout what God whispers and whisper what He shouts; that is, when we overemphasize what He doesn't, and underemphasize what He does. The truth in this verse is one that deserves to be shouted, not whispered.

Don't ever forget what we as believers are promised: *If we suffer mistreatment for doing what is right, we will receive blessings from our Father.*

To review, God asks us to submit even to harsh treatment and not defend ourselves for these main reasons:

- It makes room for God's righteous judgment.

- We might inherit a blessing.

Quoting what David wrote in Psalm 34, Peter went on to fill in more of the details:

> "He who would love life
> And see good days,

> Let him refrain his tongue from evil,
> And his lips from speaking deceit.
> Let him turn away from evil and do good;
> Let him seek peace and pursue it.
> For the eyes of the LORD are on the righteous,
> And His ears are open to their prayers;
> But the face of the LORD is against those
> who do evil. (1 Peter 3:10–12)

In other words, when you are insulted, bless back. When authority mistreats you, bless back. For in so doing you will be setting yourself up for a blessing!

The next time you are unfairly treated, especially by someone in authority, you need to call your husband or wife and spread the good news to your friends—"God is setting me up to get blessed. I can't wait to see what He's going to do!"

On the other hand, when you slip and don't respond correctly to the unfairness of others, you need to realize that something good God wants to hand over to you may have to wait awhile until you figure this out.

Do we have any idea how many blessings we have squandered because we just "had to have the last word" or "had to defend our rights" or "had to get even"? How much weeping will there be in heaven at the judgment seat because we understand what was lost when too many times you and I did not handle unfair treatment correctly?

God's Harvest

If we want to see the kingdom of God advance mightily on the earth, we need to bring in the body of Christ's harvest. God wants us to reap the blessings of His harvest. I need your harvest! You need mine! Because if every believer reaps the harvest God intends, it will bring the expansion of God's kingdom, which certainly includes souls saved!

God *wants* that. We don't want to end up standing before God in heaven and have Him say, "I had a harvest for you, and look at the implications, look at the people that did not make it here because you didn't receive your harvest! Look at the financial blessings you could have had, look at the social blessings you could have had, look at the intellectual/mental blessings you could have had." God's plan is to bless us in every area of life—spirit, soul, body, finances, possessions—every realm.

The harvest always relates to increase, not just personally, but for everyone. We see a significant beginning of this in what God promised to Abraham:

I will bless those who bless you, and I will curse him who curses you; and in you all the families of the earth shall be blessed. (Genesis 12:3)

God told Abraham that the reward for his obedience would be a personal blessing that would extend to all the families of the earth. You and I are still receiving the blessings extended to our father Abraham because he was obedient!

God blesses in many ways: "Every good gift and every perfect gift is from above, and comes down from the Father of lights" (James 1:17). Sometimes it is a financial blessing; sometimes it is wisdom or understanding. Consider John the Baptist's blessing: he was not a man of wealth or many possessions. My goodness— he lived in the wilderness, his designer clothes were animal skins, and his gourmet meals included locusts and wild honey. Yet look at the prophetic insight he was given and the authority in which he spoke. He had the honor to baptize the Savior of the world. And Jesus said of him that "among those born of women there has not risen one greater than John the Baptist" (Matt. 11:11). John brought in his harvest, and lives are still touched.

Consider Joseph of Aramathea: He was a man blessed with wealth, and he used some of it to donate the temporary tomb for our Lord. That's where the Resurrection took place! Joseph brought in his harvest. Lives are still being influenced.

All of us have different gifts, and the harvest usually will come in those areas where God has gifted us. If you are a businessman and you've been unfairly treated, your harvest is probably going to come in the area of greater business opportunities. And with that you will influence more people.

What I have noticed in my personal life, and you will too, is that the more God has blessed me, the more of an influence I've been able to have on the lives of others. We Christians need to wake up and become who we really are—heirs of the

King instead of pitiful paupers! Jesus is the King of kings, not the King of paupers! Why do the ungodly movie actors, politicians, business magnates, athletes, and pornographers like Hugh Heffner have the greatest influence today? Could it be that Christians are not appropriating the blessings God wants to give so that the harvest

> **All of us have different gifts, and the harvest usually will come in those areas where God has gifted us.**

will increase? God will give each of us what we require for our harvest. Abraham needed cattle, silver, and gold because he had a nation to build. David needed silver because he was overseeing a nation. Elijah did not need such riches because he had insight from God and a different role to play.

When God blesses you, He will bless you in the area that you are called to. And God wants to use the whole body of Christ to bring in the harvest. That's why He made some leaders and some givers and some teachers and some helpers and some _____. You fill in the blank.

Brian's Blessing

I want to share a story with you that shows how God steps up to bless when we handle mistreatment His way. This illustrates, too, how the blessings may come—often in the area of your calling. In this case, a businessman was blessed in his area of business.

I have a close friend, Al Brice, who is a pastor. Some years ago he pastored a church in Dallas and preached from 1 Peter on the same topic—"how to respond correctly to mistreatment."

When Al finished speaking at a Sunday morning service, one of the members of the church (I'll call him Brian) came up and asked a question. "Pastor Brice," he said, "I am a junior executive for a very large insurance company. Not long ago I was next in line to become vice president. All my fellow employees knew I had earned the promotion. I really deserved that job. But when the position came open, the company gave it to another man."

"Why did that happen?" Pastor Brice asked.

"Because the other man is white and I'm black. Pastor, that's discrimination. And I believe I can prove it. I can go after this in the courts. In fact, I was getting ready to start legal action this coming week. But now you preached this message this morning and messed me up!"

Pastor Brice looked at Brian and said, "Do you want to do it God's way or do you want to do it your way?"

Without hesitation Brian answered, "I want to do it God's way; that's why I'm here talking to you. Would you please pray with me?"

Al said, "Yes," and they bowed their heads and committed Brian's case into the hands of his Father, who would judge righteously.

The next morning Brian went to work and decided to pay a

visit to the fellow who had received the promotion. He went to the man's office, stuck out his hand, and said with a big smile, "I want to congratulate you on your promotion. I just want you to know I'm going to be your best worker." You can imagine how uncomfortable this made the other guy, because he knew, too, that the promotion had gone to the wrong person. Without events going the way they did, Brian would have been *his* boss and been sitting behind the same desk.

Several weeks went by and nothing happened. You need to understand—that's often the case. God's judgment or deliverance will come, but it's often later than we would prefer! But Brian did not dwell on how he had been wronged. He just kept performing his duties at a high level.

One day Brian got a call from a competitor, an extremely large international insurance company that had a branch office in Dallas. The man on the other end of the line said, "We've watched how you deal with mutual clients. We're very impressed. Would you be interested in coming to work for us?"

Brian didn't need to think long about this. "No, I'm not interested," he said. "I don't want to change jobs. I've been with this company for years. I have great benefits and a solid group of clients. My customers and fellow workers know my reputation and character. I'm in good shape. I really don't like change. Thank you, but I'm just not interested."

The man from the other company persisted: "Please, just meet us for one lunch so we can talk to you. What could be the harm in that?"

Brian tried to be even more firm: "I'm telling you, you're wasting your time. I'm not interested."

It was almost like the other guy was hard of hearing: "Oh come on! Would you just give us one lunch?"

Almost in frustration, Brian said, "All right, I'll meet with you."

A time was set and the day of the lunch arrived. Brian and the others exchanged greetings and ordered their meals. One of the executives from the large insurance company said, "Brian, we've watched you and been so impressed with the way you handle your accounts. Our people have said, 'Man, we would love for him to work for us.'"

Brian shook his head. "I told you before on the phone. You are wasting your time. I do not want to change jobs. I like stability. I have super benefits. I have so much invested with my company. I just don't want to do this."

"Okay, Brian, we hear you. But this is what we want you to do. Go home and talk to your wife. The two of you come up with a salary figure that you would like us to pay you. And then let's meet back here in a week or so and talk about it."

Almost against his better judgment, Brian sighed and said, "Well, all right."

He went home. He really had not taken any of this very seriously. He didn't even say much to his wife about the offer until the night before the next lunch. Brian was relaxing with his wife and finally said, "I really don't want to change jobs. They wanted us to name a salary figure. I'm really tired of this, so this is what I'm going to do: I'll just say the most ridiculous thing. I'll tell them I want a salary that is three times what I'm making now! That will end this fruitless discussion real quick," Brian said.

He wrote a short letter and put in the salary figure that was triple his current pay. Keep in mind that he was already quite high up in his company. Naming such a high number seemed ludicrous.

The next day Brian went to lunch. The men all sat down, and after the food was ordered, the insurance company executive asked Brian if he had come up with a salary request.

"I did," Brian said. He started to reach in his coat pocket to pull out the letter, but the other man stopped him. "No, no. We really don't want to see what you want us to pay you. We first want to show you what we want to pay you!"

The man slid a letter across the lunch table. Brian picked it up, and after reading a few lines, almost passed out. The number they were proposing was *four times* the salary he was making! Brian was so stunned that he didn't know what to say. He just sat there staring at the letter. However, the men from the other insurance company misunderstood his speechlessness and concluded that maybe their offer wasn't high enough. So they upped their salary offer considerably and added more benefits!

Finally, Brian regained his composure and said, "Gentlemen, I'm a Christian, so I want to take this offer home so I can pray about it with my wife. I'll get back with you."

"Sure, sure, take your time," the others said.

Brian went home and told his wife. They prayed, and the Spirit of God spoke to both of them. The message from the

Lord was, "Son, you put your case in My hands. I have vindicated you. This is My promotion. Take it!"

Now, almost twenty years later, Brian doesn't live in Dallas anymore. He is a top executive of that giant insurance company at their international headquarters in Virginia. This company dwarfs the company Brian was working for when he was mistreated and did not get the promotion he deserved.

What are we to conclude from this? Sure, Brian could have defended himself. He had a legitimate legal case. He had rights he could have insisted on. He had been mistreated and possibly would have won the case. Even if he had won the case, he would not have been where he is today. He would have missed the blessing he was set up for!

I must tell you that I have observed many people who have taken the course of action of defending themselves. Some of them even have won and received some justice, but their spirits were never the same. They were left with scars from the experience, and according to Scripture missed the blessings that were waiting for them.

> **We have to understand our lives from God's perspective. Nothing gets by Him.**

It's *always* best to do it God's way, just as Brian did. We have to understand our lives from God's perspective. Nothing gets by Him. He knows how many hairs are on your head, how many cells in your body. Do you not think He knows when you've been harmed by someone? Yes! Yes! Yes! God mightily protects those who let Him respond to the unfair treatment they receive.

Take a look again at what Peter wrote: "And who is he who will harm you if you become followers of what is good?" (1 Peter 3:13). What Peter was saying here is, "Hey man or woman, boy or girl, when you believe this and get it into your spirit and live this way, what can anybody do to you? How can anybody ever really take advantage of you or harm you again? They are just setting you up to get *blessed!*"

"Praise God!" is my response.

That is why Jesus said to His disciples that if someone wanted their shirt, they should give the person their coat as well. And if someone wanted them to walk a mile, they should go two miles. Of course this was radical kingdom thinking, especially for the Jews, who had been taught to take an eye for an eye. But Jesus is God. He knew the truth. This kind of life is what God wants.

My friend, you can live a life right now on earth where you will never be stolen from again. Instead, do yourself a service—have a servant's heart. A servant gives while the slave has been stolen from. Do not return evil for evil. Those who abuse you really can't do anything that will ultimately hurt you. Don't be just a slave. Be something better than that: be a servant as Jesus was a servant. You will be free—more free to live powerfully for God than ever before.

If I were preaching I would expect you to say "Amen" to that! And say it with enthusiasm!

7

Rising Above Mistreatment

I think you will agree that the goal for every Christian is to grow up! The Bible is quite clear on this topic: Remaining a spiritual baby is not good. Growing out of spiritual infancy and becoming a mature man or woman of God is what He intends for every believer. And I'm sure you will not be surprised that mistreatment is one of the prime instructional tactics God uses to help us all become spiritual adults.

Again, Peter explained how this works:

> Therefore, since Christ suffered for us in the flesh, arm your-selves also with the same mind, for he who has suffered in the flesh has ceased from sin. (1 Peter 4:1)

Another meaning for "ceased from sin" is "reached complete spiritual maturity."

The Bible describes different stages and levels of spiritual growth that bear some resemblance to what occurs to us physically.

We all start out as babies who are very dependent on parents or other adults for care. As spiritual newborn babes we are to "desire the pure milk of the word, that you may grow thereby" (1 Peter 2:2). There's nothing wrong with spiritual milk for a baby. In fact, it is perfect for a baby, because it is all an infant's spiritual digestive system can handle. But at some point every baby needs to wean off that milk and move on to more solid food.

That's why we find the Bible also talks about children: we should "no longer be children, tossed to and fro and carried about with every wind of doctrine, by the trickery of men, in the cunning craftiness of deceitful plotting" (Eph. 4:14).

And finally Scripture mentions spiritual adulthood: "Solid food belongs to those who are of full age, that is, those who by reason of use have their senses exercised to discern both good and evil" (Heb. 5:14).

I want to point out some significant differences, however, between physical and spiritual growth. Assuming other things are normal, growth of your physical body is primarily a function of time. There has never been a two-year-old who was already six feet tall. (But if there had been, you can bet college basketball recruiters would already be visiting!) Physical development like that requires at least fifteen years or more.

Intellectual growth is also different from physical growth. You can be very smart and still be quite young. Some little kids already possess incredible genius. Especially precocious students can be done with high school and in college by age fifteen. And yet some people are fifty years old and still trying to get a GED high school diploma. Intellectual development is not a function of time but of learning. You proceed from first grade to second and so on until you finish elementary school. But if you are homeschooled in a special educational environment, you can make it as long or as short as you want.

Now spiritual growth is unique from both physical and intellectual growth. It is not a matter of time. Some people born-again for just a year are spiritually tall, while others who have been Christians for decades are still spiritual tykes wearing Pampers and sucking on pacifiers. They are the ones who often do the most whining in the church and cause pastors to lose a lot of sleep!

Spiritual growth is not solely a function of knowledge, either. When Jesus came to earth, the religious hotshots of the day—the Pharisees—knew a lot of information about God and Scripture. Many of them could recite the first five books of the Bible from memory. Yet all that knowledge didn't help them recognize the Son of God when He came and stood right in front of their faces.

Today we see the same thing. There are some people who've gone through Bible school and seminary. They have studied doctrine, read all the right books, teach others, and have a theological résumé that is mighty impressive. But many of them would not recognize the Holy Spirit if He came into a service wearing a red coat and matching hat.

Spiritual maturity is not a function of just learning and time. Of course God can use education and time to assist in maturing us, but they do not guarantee it. We see in 1 Peter 4:1 what really "grows us up" in the Lord, and it is none other than suffering—and I don't mean suffering caused by our own foolishness, but suffering encountered when we are obedient to God.

Now you may be questioning: *I know people who have suffered and are bitter.* Yes, that is true because there is another key ingredient to growing. It is found in Hebrews 5:8: "Though He was a Son, yet He learned obedience by the things which He suffered." Jesus was fully God and fully Man, but as the incarnate Son of God, He still needed to learn what it meant to obey His Father here on earth.

> **Many would not recognize the Holy Spirit if He came into a service wearing a red coat and matching hat.**

How do we grow spiritually? When we go through unfair treatment, affliction, and persecution and still choose to obey. It is easy to obey when the sun's shining, you're sitting in church with your family and friends, or you're at a Christian seminar or conference. When everybody likes you and life just couldn't get any better, being obedient seems almost as easy and natural as breathing. But when the hurricane comes, when people are criticizing you, when your boss has you in his doghouse, when friends are maligning you, when nothing seems to go right—if you still choose to be obedient then and bless your enemies by giving to them when it's not deserved, that's when obedience really counts for something.

Forgive . . . As You Have Been Forgiven

There is one area in your life that perhaps more than any other can be a huge barrier to becoming fully mature and having the ability to respond with grace to those who mistreat you: unforgiveness.

Let's face it, there are many situations in life where we have been mistreated that just do not resolve cleanly enough to leave us with peace in our spirits. And even though we fully intend to obey God and not return "evil for evil," the sting of hurt lodged in our hearts refuses to leave. At that point we must do what Jesus asked us to do—forgive. I don't have all the answers to why this is so important to God, but it certainly is. There will be precious little spiritual power unleashed in our lives if we hang on tightly to offense. Responding well to the unfair treatment we receive is not just a mental exercise. It is deeply spiritual, must come from our hearts, and by its very nature will require us to forgive. Like Jesus we have to be able to say, "Forgive them, for they know not what they do." This is the key to stopping the urge to defend yourself: you forgive.

> **This is the key to stopping the urge to defend yourself: you forgive.**

So how can you forgive—perhaps even the most outrageous mistreatment? With God's help, you must reach a point first where you understand what you've been forgiven of yourself. Your sin—my sin—required Jesus to die on that cross. We are guilty of every sin imaginable, including the unjust execution of the Son of God. For that the sentence is eternal torment in hell. If God can forgive us for such crimes, then there's nothing—let me say it again—*nothing* we cannot forgive someone for doing to us.

We have been shown great mercy. In obedience and love we need to extend the same mercy to others.

Get Armed

When the Bible says that those who have suffered in the flesh "have ceased from sin," it means that such a person is no longer in bondage to habitual sins.

Again, here's how Peter summarized it:

Therefore, since Christ suffered for us in the flesh, arm yourselves also with the same mind, for he who has suffered in the flesh has ceased from sin. (1 Peter 4:1)

First, did you notice the word *therefore*? In Scripture it always means, "Get ready; here comes the conclusion to what's been said before." Peter had just devoted three chapters in his letter explaining how we are to respond to mistreatment and endure suffering. Then he gave us the bottom line.

There is so much energizing truth in this verse. To begin with Peter said, "Since Christ suffered for us in the flesh." Now, just how did Christ suffer in the flesh? For one thing He received almost constant *unfair treatment!* I explained that in chapter 3.

Then Peter informed us that this is what we also will endure—we need to "arm" ourselves or get ready for suffering mistreatment. As we discovered earlier, this is what we are called to do.

Honestly, since I became a Christian, I've had more trials than I ever had before. In many ways life was easier back then; but I also was blind to reality, because before I met Jesus I was a prisoner held captive by Satan. Which type of life appeals most to you? Would you choose to be a POW, locked in a cage with your hands tied, or would you rather be the guy free to forward the cause of his country by advancing on an evil army that is holding many POWs? The guy in the POW camp is a prisoner; the guy getting shot at is a free man. When I was in the world and not a believer, I was a prisoner and didn't have as many trials. I'm free now, but guess who's getting shot at? And I bet you are under fire, too. Welcome to real life!

> When I was in the world and not a believer, I was a prisoner and didn't have as many trials. I'm free now, but guess who's getting shot at?

The suffering that Peter was saying Christ endured was unfair treatment from those in authority, as well as from others. Over and over He was wrongfully accused and did not defend Himself. Peter said that we must prepare to do the same, so we better get armed or prepared.

What would you have thought of President George W. Bush if he had ordered American troops to fight a war in Iraq but had not supplied them with air support, tanks, artillery, rifles, ammunition, knives—all the supplies required to win a battle? You rightly would have thought that not properly equipping an army was the height of foolishness. Defeat would be a sure thing. No nation expecting victory would ever send its military into battle without arms. But in a similar way, this is exactly what happens when Christians are not armed to suffer unfair treatment. Sadly, many are not!

I have ministered to believers throughout America and all over the world. I have observed over and over that Christians have not been taught how to prepare for mistreatment and suffering. The Christian life has many benefits, but it is a soldier's life. And God commands that we do this correctly for His glory. So when the pressure comes, most Christians—because they are like soldiers sent to the battlefield without rifles or ammunition—become bewildered and amazed and go into a state of shock when someone wrongs them. Instead of knowing how to *act* as Jesus did, they *react*. We believers need to prepare, to arm ourselves with the right kind of information and the Spirit's power so that when we are hit with unfair treatment, we know how to respond.

A good example of such training is what commercial airline pilots do on a regular basis. Every six months or so these men and women are pulled from regular flights by the airlines for about three days and trained on flight simulators. These machines are amazing, kind of a mix of an amusement-park ride, high-tech video game, and sophisticated computer software. When the pilots climb inside the simulated flight deck, it's as though they were on board a real aircraft. All of the gauges and controls are the same. When the pilots look out the windows, they see just what they would if they were taxiing, flying, or landing their aircraft—runways, earth and sky, a variety of weather conditions, wind shear—the whole deal. And that's not all. Everything they might feel—turbulence, wind, the sensations of climbing or diving—it's all programmed in. The simulator feels and responds just like a real aircraft.

> **The Christian life has many benefits, but it is a soldier's life.**

For three days the instructors and testing personnel throw every catastrophic event imaginable at the pilots in that flight simulator. When the pilots encounter a situation they are not familiar with, often they crash. That means they get to try again, crash after crash, until they learn how to get it right and keep the plane aloft. Then if a similar situation ever develops on a real flight, the pilots will know how to respond—instantaneously.

This is why when an airplane does go down in a crash and the black boxes and voice recorders are recovered, the tapes may reveal that the passengers in the main cabin were screaming. They were not *armed* or prepared, so all they do is *react* in fear. But the recording of the pilots will reveal them calmly saying, "Do this, check, feather the engines, check, check, pull up, check, check, check, got this, check, check, check." They are *acting*, not *reacting*. Usually the pilots are calm and cool all the way to the crash. Sure, if they can't stop what's happening, they may let out a cussword. But that's it. They are absolutely in control the whole way down. The pilots are *armed*.

Most believers are not *armed* to handle mistreatment.

What I am doing in this book is giving you the training. You're in the simulator! I'm arming you now from the Word of God with how our Maker wants us to respond when people and life fling harsh, unfair things in our faces. We want to know how to do it right so that we honor our King and do not miss out on a single blessing!

8

Will He Find Faith?

If you are like me, you don't want to be a spiritual weakling. Instead you want to have spiritual muscles that you can flex and do some kingdom lifting when you are confronted with mistreatment or any other challenge that requires you to be able to push back the darkness and advance the cause of Christ here on earth.

Gaining Strength

I like to compare what needs to happen to us spiritually with some of my own experience in gaining strength physically.

Back in the mid-1990s, I was really kind of a skinny runt. Because I have always had such a high metabolism, if I don't watch myself, I end up underweight. (Believe me, I'm not whining about this. I know many people have the opposite problem!) Back then I was probably at least twenty pounds under my ideal, healthy weight. I was so weak and lacking in stamina that my ability to preach was affected. One Sunday morning I was standing on the platform before I was to give the message and I became kind of dizzy and saw stars. That's how worn out I was; I hadn't even gotten up to start preaching and I wondered if I was going to pass out.

Because she was concerned, Lisa had been talking to me about my need to take better care of myself; she had prayed for months that I would do something about my health. So after this Sunday-morning incident, I came home and said to her, "That does it; I'm going to start working out."

Thankfully, God had placed a neighbor next door to us who was a WWF wrestler. We had become close to this family. So I went to this guy and said, "Would you be willing to give me some physical training?" He said that he would be happy to, so I put on my sweats and we started going to the gym three times a week.

We must have made a funny-looking pair, because he was a huge mound of muscle—six foot four, 279 pounds, and just 6 percent body fat. His arms were as big as my legs.

It didn't take long before I learned how you go about building muscle mass. I found out that you get in better shape by pumping some weight for twelve repetitions. But if you really want to see your muscles bulge, you put way more weight on the bar and give it all you've got to lift that thing a couple of times. And then when your muscles are screaming and everything inside you says, "I can't do this," you pour every last bit of strength into hoisting the bar one more time.

So there I was—"Mr. Universe Not"—a bit on the skinny, weak side, watching this massive wrestler and his monster buddies at the gym. They would be sitting on the bench loudly urging each other on, "Lift it, push, explode, come on!" and a guy would let out a grunt and start to strain, his blood vessels bulging and face red. He'd give a mighty push and up the weight would go.

So of course that's what my neighbor wanted me to do. "That's how you'll get strong, John," he said. "You have to get to the place when you say, 'There's no way I can push it up one more time!' But something on the inside of you drives it up; that's when muscle grows."

What in the world have I gotten myself into? I wondered.

But I just didn't want to be weak anymore. So I started lifting weights, and it was pathetic. At first I could bench only 95 pounds. But my friend and I kept going to the gym, and before long I made it to 105 pounds. After a week or two more, I made it to 115 pounds. With his encouragement I stayed at it and started increasing—125, 135, 145, 155, 165, 175, 185. This did not happen overnight; it took a couple of years to make it to this point. But then I got stuck. It seemed to me I just had maxed myself out.

I was speaking at a conference in Fresno, California, once during this time; and some of the pastors took me along to their gym. While we were working out and lifting weights, one of them said to me, "John, you can bench 225 pounds, no problem."

"Are you crazy? I can't do anywhere near 225."

"Sure you can. Get on the bench; I'll spot you."

"You're crazy; I can't do this," I said. I wasn't exactly filled with faith.

But the pastor got me to the bench, loaded the weights, then spotted me and urged me on. Unbelievably, I pushed that bar up. I went *nuts!* I really could hardly believe it.

Later that day we went out to lunch. We were eating, and I said to this pastor friend, "You know what? For me you're like the Holy Spirit."

"What?" he said, giving me a puzzled look.

"Don't you remember what the Bible says?" I asked him. "'No temptation has overtaken you except such as is common to man; but God is faithful, *who will not allow you to be tempted beyond what you are able,* but with the temptation will also make the way of escape, that you may be able to bear it'" (1 Cor. 10:13, emphasis added).

My pastor friend started seeing it. The Holy Spirit knows what we are able to bear, and most often it's more than we think we can handle.

"You knew I could lift 225 pounds," I said. "You knew I could bear it!"

His encouragement and faith in my ability helped me break the barrier holding me back. Not too many months later I went to 235, but got stuck again.

A year or so later, I got to work out with one of the top power-lifting coaches in the United States, and the guy said to me, "You can do 275, no sweat."

Here we go again! I thought. I immediately replied, "You're crazy!"

He laughed, and after a few warm-ups and some good tips,

I pushed up 256 pounds! I was so excited I called my wife in celebration.

Several months later I was with the same coach again. (He attends a church in Detroit, Michigan, where the senior pastor can bench-press over 455 pounds!) I had just preached the entire Sunday on being sensitive to the Holy Spirit. Monday morning this coach looked at me and said, "John, I had a dream last night that you benched over 300 pounds."

I laughed at him as if he were out of his mind. But the senior pastor and he both reminded me of what I had preached the day before. I conceded and said, "Let's go for it."

We did the warm-ups, and he progressively moved up to the mark. I pushed up the 300 pounds. He then said, "Now let's do 315."

He put it on and spotted me and sure enough, the 315 pounds went up unassisted (it's the first and probably the last time I'll do that).

In regard to my physical fitness and muscle strength, these two weightlifting coaches are like the Holy Spirit in the spiritual realm: They often know what you can handle better than yourself. This reminds me of what the Holy Spirit had the author of Hebrews write—"by this time you ought to be teachers"—but he chided them and said that they were weaklings and needed to go back to drinking milk instead of solid food (see Heb. 5:12).

So in effect the Lord has to say to us, "All right, let's start getting you back in shape. I've got something I want you to do for Me, and it is going to carry 105 pounds of mistreatment with it, but you are ready!" Then somebody says something nasty to you, and you can't quite bear it and snap back and defend yourself. And God says, "Okay, we need to go back down to 95 pounds again. Maybe I can give you some 'child thing' to do, but nothing more."

Maybe in your life your spiritual maturity is the equivalent of 125 pounds. God has something He desires, but it will carry a weight of persecution on your bar that demands you lift 145. In so many words He says, "I have a 145-pound job that needs to be done in the Spirit." So you get treated unfairly by an

> "I've got something I want you to do for Me, and it is going to carry 105 pounds of mistreatment with it, but you are ready!"

authority figure, and you whine and complain and don't get the job done. So God says, "Back to 125."

Maybe later the Lord says, "I need someone to handle a 155-pound lift in the Spirit. I think you can do it." So a friend betrays you or your boss gives the promotion to someone else. And instead of not returning evil for evil and standing steady, you return insult for insult and resign from your job in a huff. God says, "Back to 125."

Or God says, "I need a church that can handle a 225-pound job in the city." But the church runs into opposition and persecution, such as the newspaper running an unfavorable article. The leadership backs off. God says, "Back to 125."

Your spiritual Coach, the Holy Spirit, who is helping you train, is saying, "You should be benching 245 or 285 or 300 pounds!" But because you keep defending yourself or getting your back up when someone in authority critiques you, your Coach constantly has to take you back down to 125 pounds. You are not growing in strength. You are not obeying the commandment to bear suffering gracefully and leave vengeance in the hands of God. And though He is patient because He loves you so much, He is saying to you, "My precious child, you're just passing up your chance to grow. I have some kingdom jobs out there that require someone who can lift more than 125 pounds. Please bring in your harvest! You just passed up an opportunity to take on a 185-pounder. But you would not be able to handle it."

You are not alone in this struggle to gain spiritual muscle! I know from personal experience.

Years ago, when that administrative pastor maligned me and slandered my name all over our church, I felt like the world was caving in on me. I thought I could not bear it, that I was going out of my mind. This was my world. It looked like everything was crumbling. I had left my career in engineering to go into ministry. The burden was about all I could "lift." I really didn't understand it at the time, but that was about a 125-pounder.

But I stayed with my spiritual training. As each year passed I was strong enough spiritually to take more. Then almost twelve years after that earlier incident when I was a youth pastor, I was maligned and my name was slandered on three different continents by what a man with a huge church in Europe said about me. If this level of heavy attack had happened when I was just barely pushing 125 pounds, the bar would have fallen on me and busted every rib. It would have been like piling on 315 pounds when I first started lifting with my wrestling neighbor. It could have killed me.

By God's grace and the strength the Holy Spirit placed in me, I was able to not defend myself against these unwarranted statements. I was able to truly love the guy and continue to bless him. That kept me from allowing the poison of being offended to sicken and weaken my spirit. And in time God took care of the matter. I weep at this, but not too long after his accusation against me, this man's church went through a huge split. That ministry has not been the same since. The church lost much of its influence.

Do you want to know why Green Berets and Navy SEALs get so much respect? Because their training is so much tougher than what others in the military receive. But when tough jobs need to be done, these are the guys who get the call.

Just like the muscles in your body really grow only when your coach brings you to realms where you think you can't go, so our spiritual muscles and strength grow when the Holy Spirit asks us to push beyond our comfort zone and radically obey what God wants. He knows what we can bear! But we have to trust Him enough to push ourselves to accomplish the heavy work of the kingdom.

God's Way, or Man's Way?

God weeps because we refuse to do things His way. He is saying, "Hey, Christians, I've got some tough jobs that need doing on earth. The harvest is plentiful, and the laborers are few. My people are worried about what others are thinking or saying about them or that their boss said something critical about them. They are standing up for their rights. But there are people dying and going to hell. I need people positioned who can handle 175, 185, 200, 225, 250, 300, 350-pound tasks!"

> Our spiritual muscles and strength grow when the Holy Spirit asks us to push beyond our comfort zone and radically obey what God wants.

Jesus said that in the last days offense would run rampant in the world. The Greek word for *many* means "the majority," and what's really scary is that He wasn't talking about people in society—He was talking about Christians when He said, "And then many will be offended, will betray one another, and will hate one another" (Matt. 24:10).

The result of all this trouble caused by the inability of believers to properly handle offenses will lead to lawlessness, which means they will not be submitted to authority. And ultimately "the love of many will grow cold" (Matt. 24:12).

Jesus closely linked insubordination to authority and offense. He said many will be offended and will betray and hate one another. That will lead to the rise of false prophets who will rise up and "deceive many" (Matt. 24:11). The many He was referring to are those who are offended! The result: "lawlessness will abound" (Matt. 24:12).

Why will lawlessness abound? It's related to all we've learned in this book. Individuals say, "Well, I've been offended. This leader did this to me or that person did that to me." And as life goes on, whenever they meet up with someone who reminds them of the person that did such and such to them before, the defenses and protective mechanisms rise into place: "I've been hurt; I'm not going to get hurt again!"

I've been in full-time ministry since 1983, and I've been traveling all over the world since 1990. I have seen many Christians who chose to defend themselves when mistreated, and in a sense, in a particular situation they "won." But I've noticed something about them. The fire for God and life isn't there. The tenderness is gone. The humility is hard to find. In taking over God's job to defend themselves and bring about justice, they forfeited something so precious and valuable. They were deceived, thinking they had gotten good results. But they missed the greater blessing—growing in strength and seeing more of the character of Christ developed in themselves.

So let's bring together the three main reasons why God tells us to not avenge or defend ourselves:

1. It makes room for God's righteous judgment.

2. We might inherit a blessing.

3. It develops the character and maturity of Christ in us.

Will He Find Us Faithful?

As this little book comes to a close, I want to issue a final challenge to you: Will you trust God enough to obey Him in how you respond to mistreatment and join with millions of others in advancing His kingdom and bringing glory to His precious name? Will you trust Him to take care of you and grant you justice in His timing—in this life or the next? Will you be one of those found faithful?

> Then He spoke a parable to them, that men always ought to pray and not lose heart, saying: "There was in a certain city a judge who did not fear God nor regard man. Now there was a widow in that city; and she came to him, saying, 'Get justice for me from my adversary.' And he would not for a while; but afterward he said within himself, 'Though I do not fear God nor regard man, yet because this widow troubles me I will avenge her, lest by her continual coming she weary me.'" Then the Lord said, "Hear what the unjust judge said. And shall God not *avenge* His own elect who cry out day and night to Him, though He bears long with them? I tell you that *He will avenge them speedily.* Nevertheless, when the Son

of Man comes, *will He really find faith on the earth?*" (Luke 18:1–8, emphasis added)

Often this parable is used to illustrate the importance of being fervent and persistent in prayer. But the last part of the parable is often ignored: "I tell you that He will avenge them speedily. Nevertheless, when the Son of Man comes, will He really find faith on the earth?"

That statement really is the core message of this book: It takes faith to not fight back when you really are mistreated by somebody—to place yourself in the hands of God instead of avenging yourself.

Praise God! We don't have to try to do this in our own strength! There is nothing that's impossible with God.

When that pastor in Europe mistreated me by slandering my reputation, and I heard it on three continents, I went to one of the men on our ministry's board, Pastor Al Brice, and asked him, "How am I doing? This is really tough! I think I'm handling this right, but what do you think?"

Because Al is also my friend and loves me, he was furious at the accusations. But Al is a man obedient to the Word of God. He knows how we are supposed to respond when mistreated. So after he calmed down, he assured me I was doing the right thing and then with a smile he said, "John, when you get in situations like this, learn from Mr. Moon."

"What do you mean?" I said. I didn't think he was referring to Reverend Moon! But I was baffled by his wisdom.

"John," Al continued, "every month the moon comes up in full, and every coyote, every wolf, every dog comes out and howls at it. But does the moon answer any of them? No! It just keeps shining." I was now registering what he was saying.

He smiled and said, "John, just keep shining!"

He then said, "Just keep preaching the pure Word of God, obey Him fully, and love people."

I urge the same of you. When offenses come, when you are mistreated and must suffer like our Lord Jesus, do one thing: *Just keep shining!*

About the Author

John Bevere is a best-selling author and popular conference speaker. He and his wife, Lisa, also a best-selling author, founded John Bevere Ministries in 1990. The ministry has grown into a multifaceted international outreach that includes their weekly television program, *The Messenger*, which broadcasts in 214 nations. John has authored numerous books, including *Drawing Near, A Heart Ablaze, Under Cover, The Bait of Satan,* and *The Fear of the Lord.* He and Lisa live in Colorado with their four sons.

Please contact us today to receive your free copy of Messenger International's *Messenger* newsletter and our 24 page color catalog of ministry resources!

The vision of MI is to strengthen believers, awaken the lost and captive in the church and proclaim the knowledge of His glory to the nations. John and Lisa are reaching millions of people each year through television and by ministering at churches, bible schools and conferences around the world. We long to see God's Word in the hands of leaders and hungry believers in every part of the earth.

MESSENGER INTERNATIONAL
www.johnbevere.org
with John and Lisa Bevere

The *Messenger* television program broadcasts in 214 countries. Some of the major networks include The God Digital Network in Europe, the Australian Christian Channel and on the New Life Channel in Russia. Please check your local listings for day and time.

UNITED STATES
PO Box 888
Palmer Lake, CO 80133-0888
800-648-1477 (US & Canada)
Tel: 719-487-3000
Fax: 719-487-3300
E-mail: jbm@johnbevere.org

EUROPE
PO Box 622
Newport, NP19 8ZJ
UNITED KINGDOM
Tel: 44 (0) 870-745-5790
Fax: 44 (0) 870-745-5791
E-mail: jbmeurope@johnbevere.org

AUSTRALIA
PO Box 6200
Dural, D.C. NSW 2158
Australia
In AUS 1-300-650-577
Tel: +61 2 8850 1725
Fax +61 2 8850 1735
Email: jbmaustralia@johnbevere.org

Other Books by John

A Heart Ablaze
The Bait of Satan
Breaking Intimidation
The Devil's Door
Drawing Near
The Fear of the Lord
Thus Saith the Lord?
Under Cover
Victory in the Wilderness
The Voice of One Crying

Books by Lisa

Be Angry, but Don't Blow It!
Kissed the Girls and Made Them Cry
Out of Control and Loving It
The True Measure of a Woman
You Are Not What You Weigh

ADDITIONAL MINISTRY RESOURCES

BOOKS • AUDIO CDs • DVDs • AUDIO CASSETTES • VHS • CURRICULUMS

*(All MI Products not shown)

Call us today and ask about our **Value Packs!** 1-800-648-1477 (US & Canada)
Australia: +61 2 8850 1725 • *Europe:* 44 (0) 870-745-5790

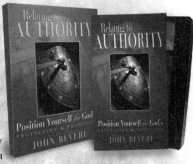
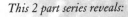

UNDER COVER

This kit contains:

- Best Selling Book, *Under Cover*
- A Leader's Guide
- A Student Workbook
- 5 VHS Tapes
- 2 DVDs
- 6 Audio CDs.

The Promise of Protection Under His Authority

Are you living under the shadow of the Almighty where there is liberty, provision, and protection? *Under Cover* is a life-transforming message that will revolutionize the way you see authority. Most people try to use kingdom principles with a democratic mindset and the kingdom of God is not a democracy, it is a kingdom with rank, order and authority. The majority of people in America do not like the subject of authority but I believe as we go through these twelve lessons and you listen carefully, you will find that you not only like authority, you will develop a passion to seek it and live it in your own life.

Dear John,

†Testimony

We have been studying your "Under Cover" series for the last several weeks in our home Life Group. Honestly, I dreaded the start of the series and even laughed inwardly with a "yeah, right" when you spoke in the first session about having a strong desire to be obedient and under authority by the end of the last tape. Well, we have finished the series, and I am blown away! Never, in my 8 years of being a Christian have I heard such a powerful and life changing message. I realized the rampant rebellion I had in my heart and my life has been transformed. My entire life group has been dramatically touched by this teaching!

- T.H., TX

This curriculum is perfect for Individual or Group Study

Family Bible Studies • Home Fellowship Groups • Church Services or Educational Programs • Bible School Curriculum • Individual Studies • Group Studies

Rise Above UNFAIR TREATMENT

This powerful video reveals:

- *Jesus' response to unfair treatment*
- *The guarantee of justice*
- *How to position ourselves for God's vindication*

We've all had this treatment; the question remains, where will it take us? We will either soar to new heights or be taken down by the storm.

Have you been mistreated by someone in authority over you? Have you felt misunderstood? Are you overwhelmed by all this? Have you been blamed for someone else's mistake? Have you felt no one knew your side of the story? If you answered yes to any of these questions, this message is for you. Too often we fall into the victim or vengeance trap. We seek to get even, and in so doing, forsake God's promise of vindication. Can protection and vindication be found? According to God's Word it is promised to those who walk in His counsel.

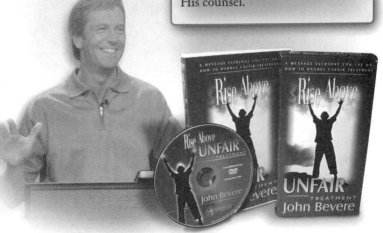